BEATLES FAVORITES

FIVE 5 FINGER PIANO

CONTENTS

This publication is not for sale in
the EU and/or Australia
or New Zealand.

ISBN 978-0-7935-9261-6

HAL•LEONARD®
CORPORATION

7777 W. BLUEMOUND RD. P.O. BOX 13819 MILWAUKEE, WI 53213

Visit Hal Leonard Online at
www.halleonard.com

All My Loving
from A HARD DAY'S NIGHT

Words and Music by John Lennon
and Paul McCartney

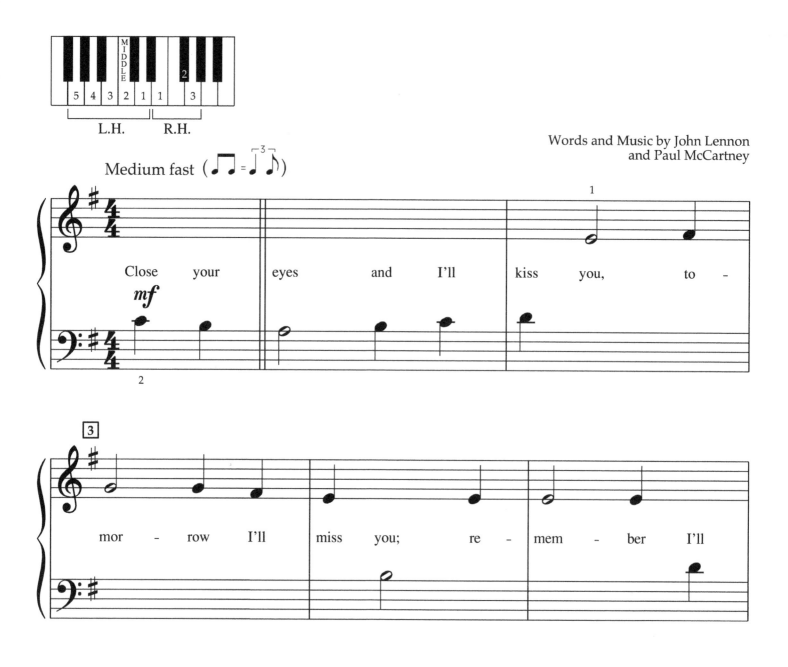

Duet Part (Student plays one octave higher than written.)

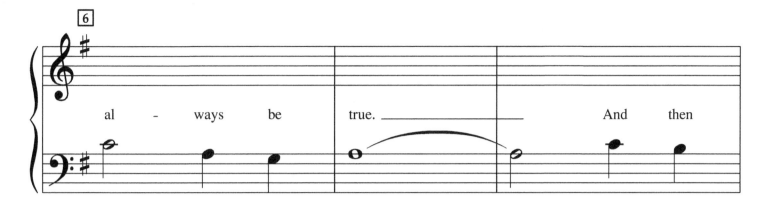

al - ways be true. _____ And then

while I'm a - way I'll write home ev - 'ry

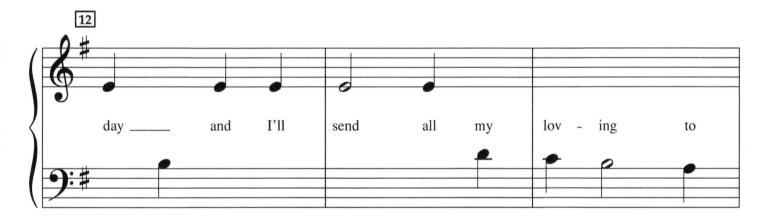

day _____ and I'll send all my lov - ing to

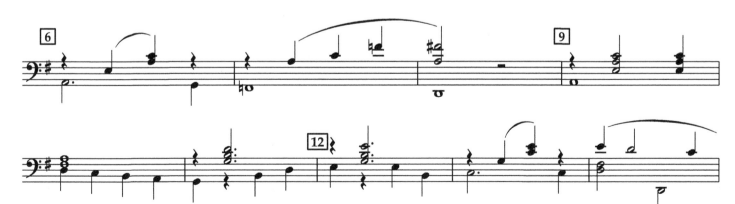

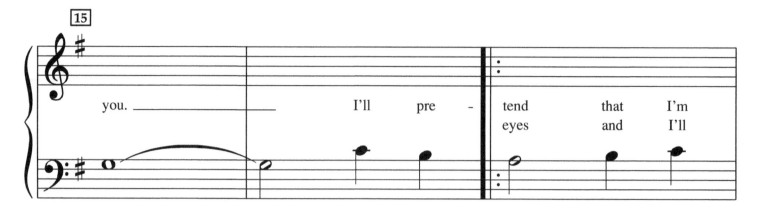

you. _____ I'll pre - tend that I'm
eyes and I'll

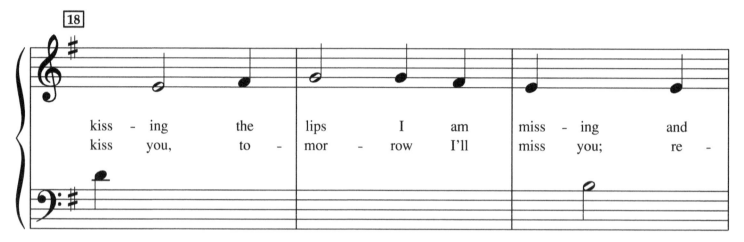

kiss - ing the lips I am miss - ing and
kiss you, to - mor - row I'll miss you; re -

hope that my dreams will come true. _____
mem - ber I'll al - ways be true. _____

4

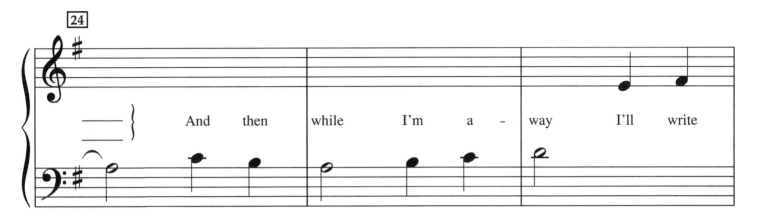

And then while I'm a - way I'll write

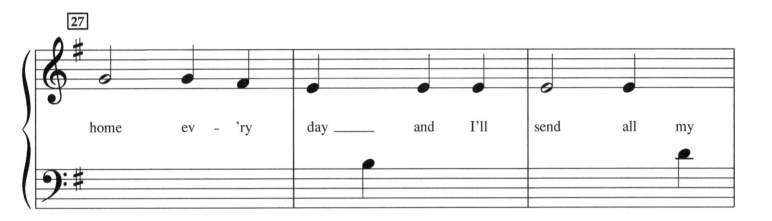

home ev - 'ry day _____ and I'll send all my

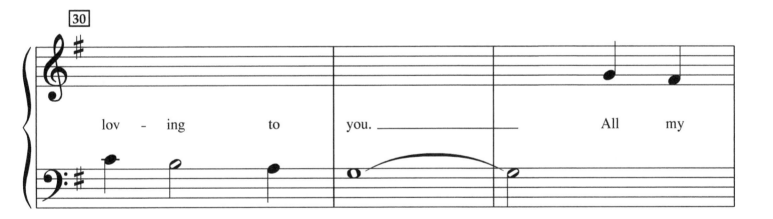

lov - ing to you. _____ All my

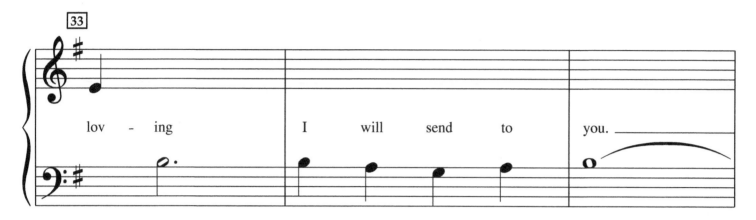

lov - ing   I   will   send   to   you. _____

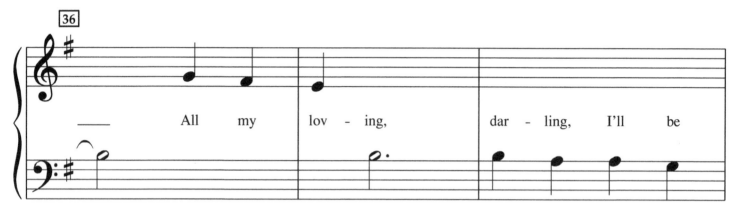

_____ All   my   lov - ing,   dar - ling,   I'll   be

1.   2.

true. _____ _____   Close   your   true. _____ _____

All You Need Is Love

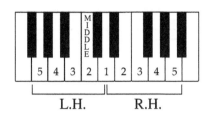

Words and Music by John Lennon
and Paul McCartney

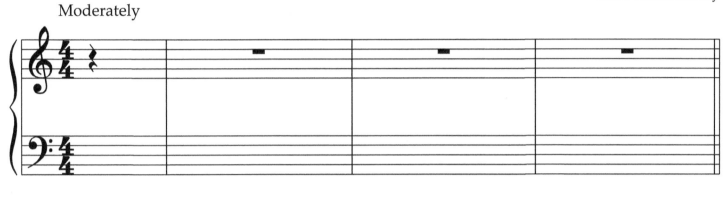

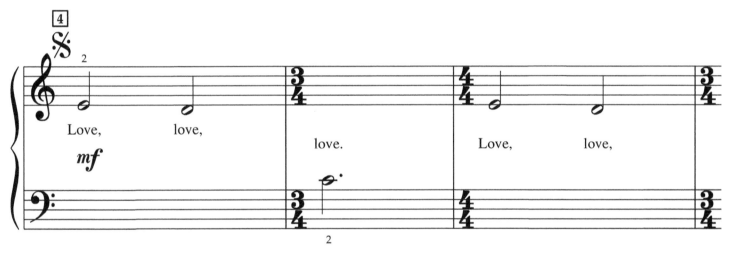

Duet Part (Student plays one octave higher than written.)

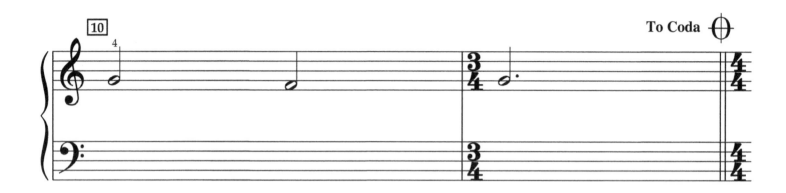

love.   Love,   love,   love.   *(Instrumental)*

To Coda

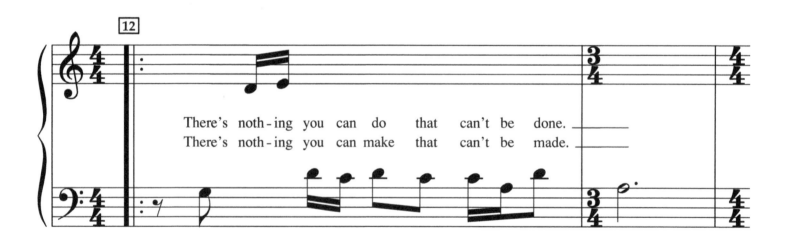

There's noth-ing you can do   that   can't be   done.
There's noth-ing you can make   that   can't be   made.

To Coda

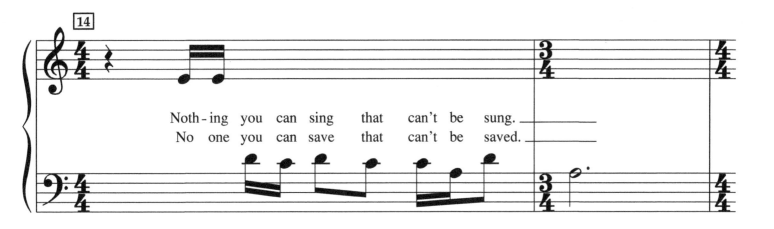

Noth - ing you can sing that can't be sung. ___
No one you can save that can't be saved. ___

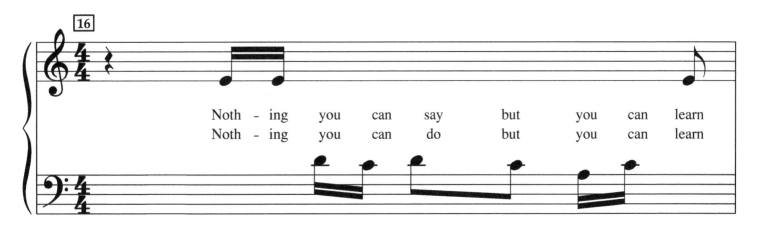

Noth - ing you can say but you can learn
Noth - ing you can do but you can learn

1.

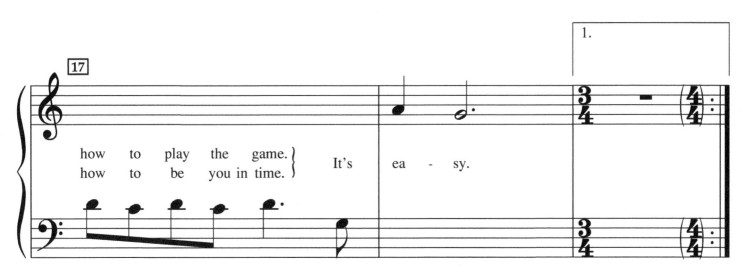

how to play the game.
how to be you in time. It's ea - sy.

1.

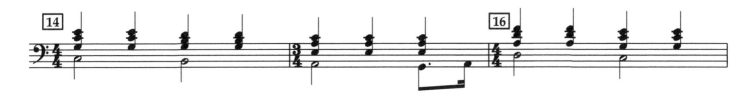

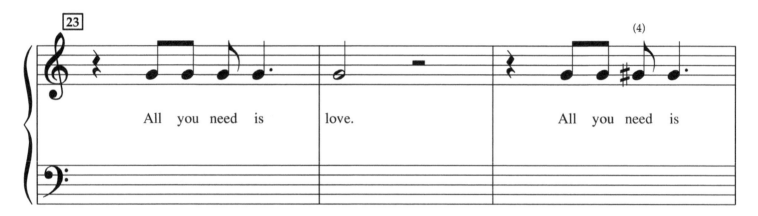

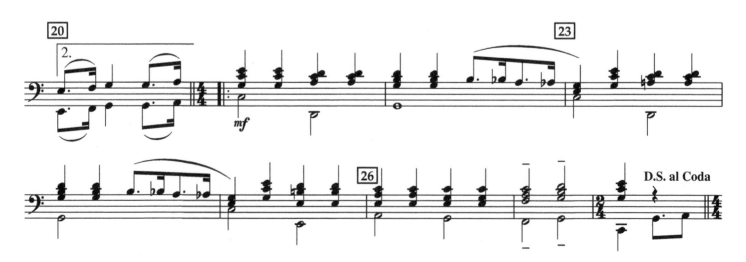

All you need is love.

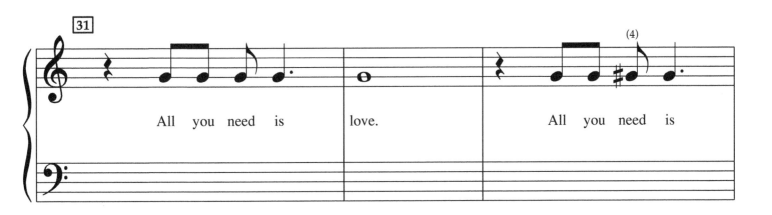

All you need is love.

All you need is

love. Love.

Love is all you need.

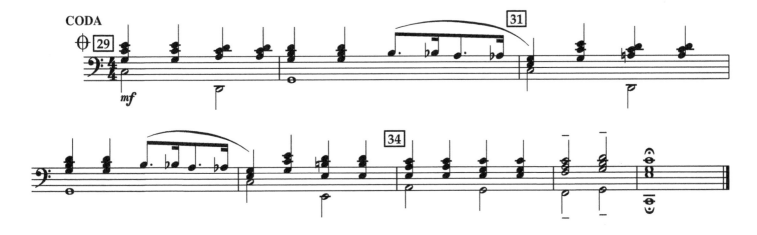

And I Love Her
from A HARD DAY'S NIGHT

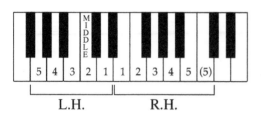

L.H.   R.H.

Words and Music by John Lennon
and Paul McCartney

Medium Rock Ballad beat

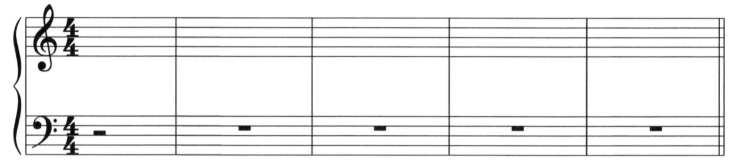

I give her all my love, that's all I do. ____

Duet Part (Student plays one octave higher than written.)
Medium Rock Ballad beat

With pedal

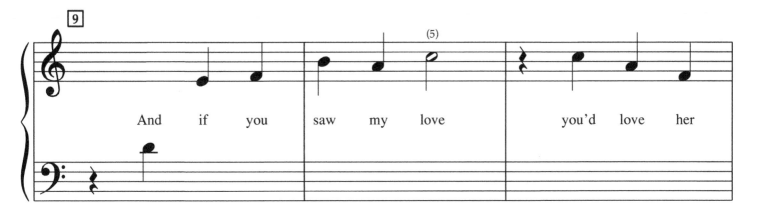

And if you saw my love you'd love her

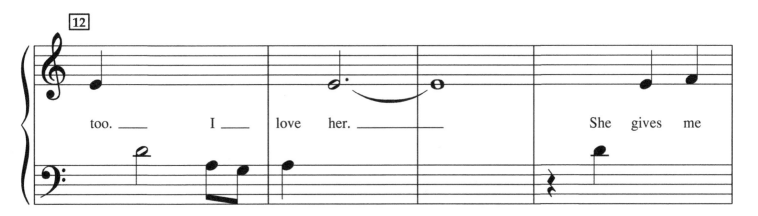

too. ____ I ____ love her. ____ She gives me

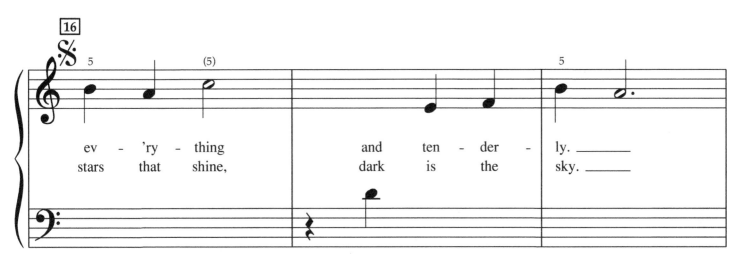

ev - 'ry - thing and ten - der - ly. ____
stars that shine, dark is the sky. ____

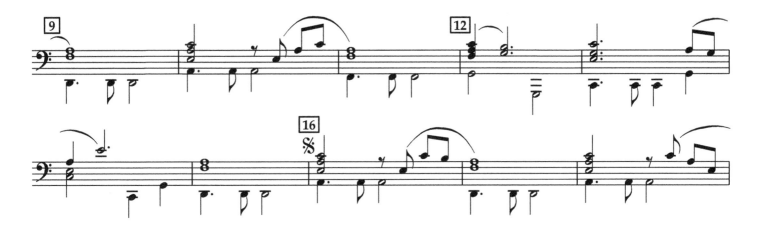

13

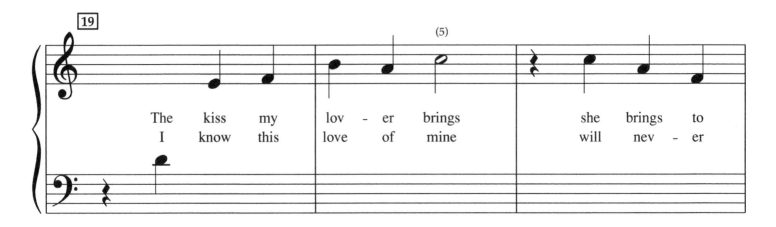

The kiss my lov - er brings she brings to
I know this love of mine will nev - er

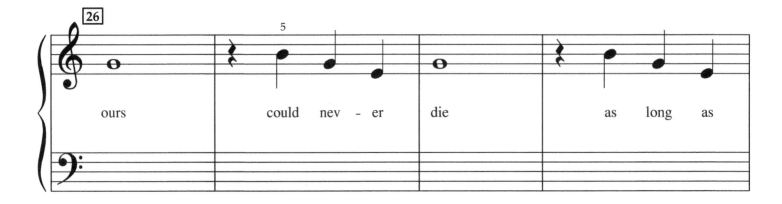

me. ___ And I love her.
die. ___ And I love her.

A love like

To Coda ⊕

ours could nev - er die as long as

To Coda ⊕

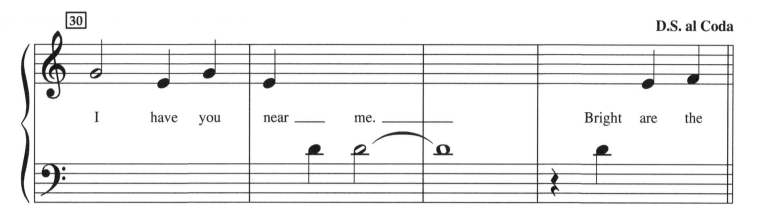

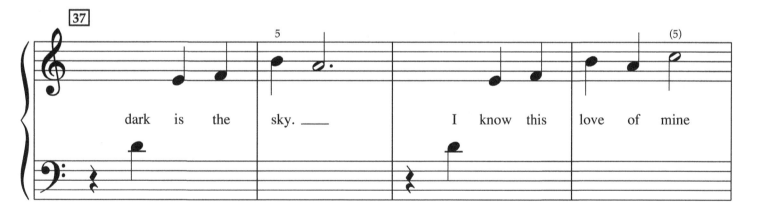

will nev – er die. ____ And I *Solo ends*

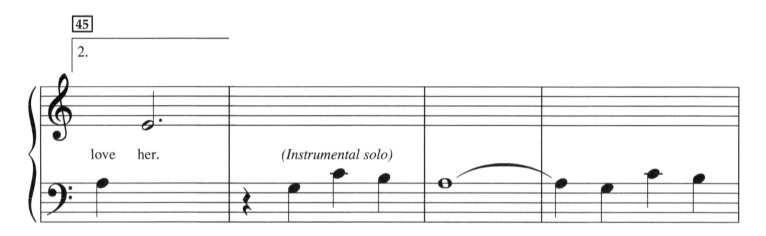

2.

love her. *(Instrumental solo)*

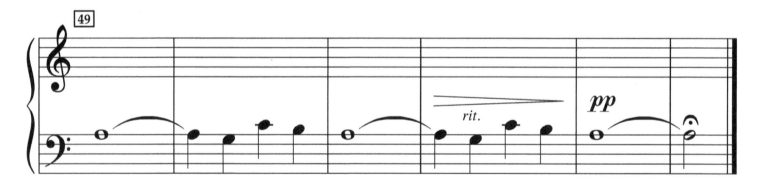

rit. **pp**

rit. **ppp**

I Want to Hold Your Hand

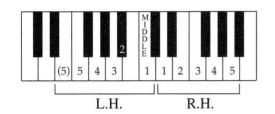

L.H.   R.H.

Words and Music by John Lennon
and Paul McCartney

Moderate Rock beat

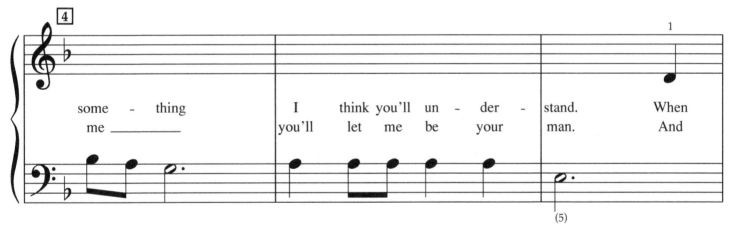

Duet Part (Student plays one octave higher than written.)
Moderate Rock beat

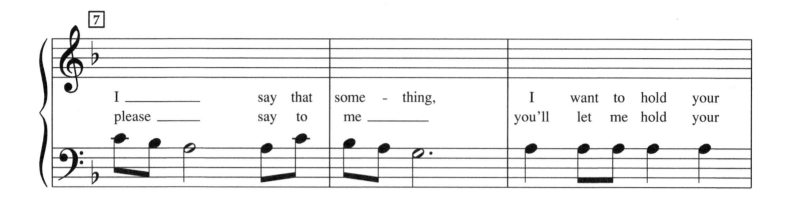

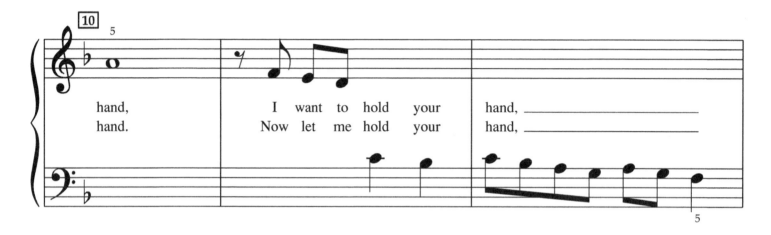

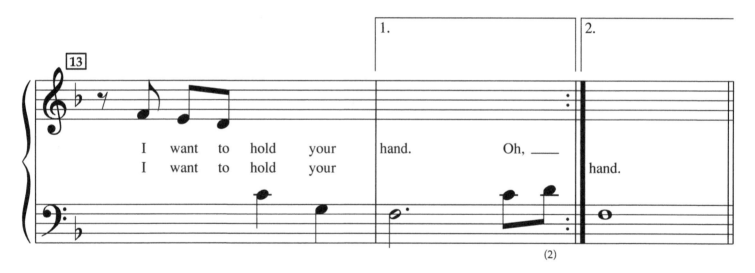

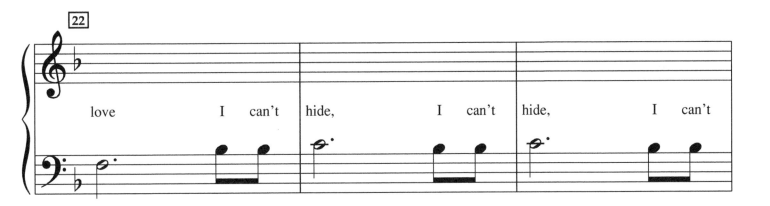

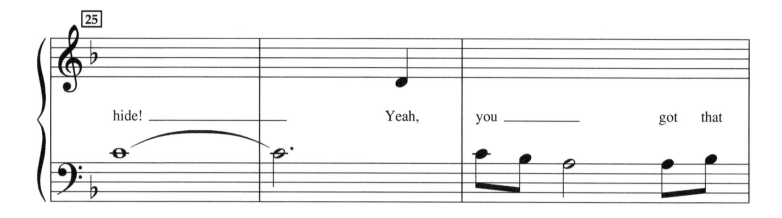

hide! _____ Yeah, you _____ got that

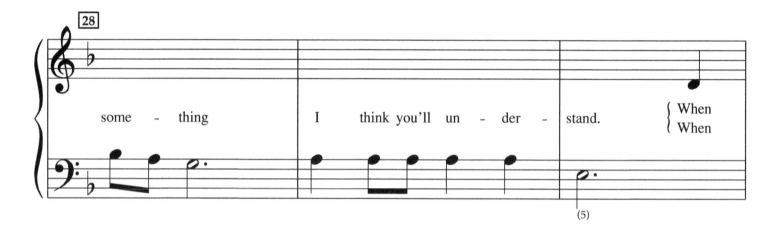

some - thing I think you'll un - der - stand. When / When

(5)

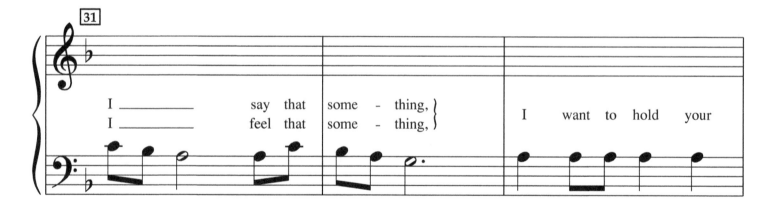

I _____ say that some - thing, } / I _____ feel that some - thing, } I want to hold your

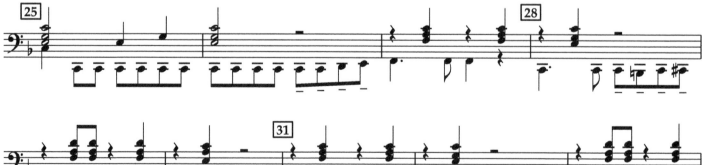

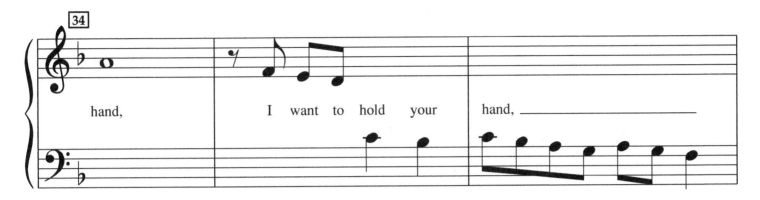

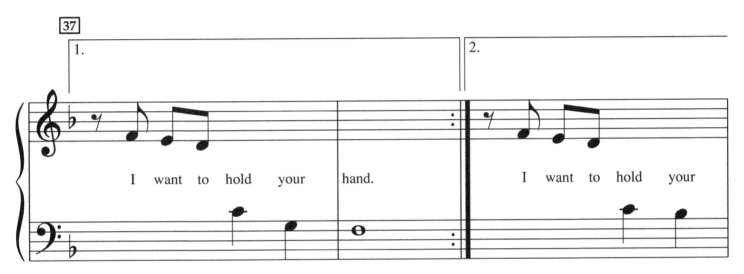

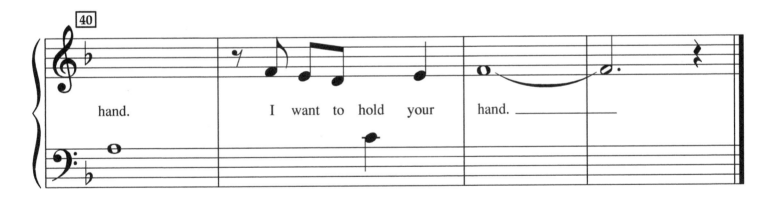

Good Night

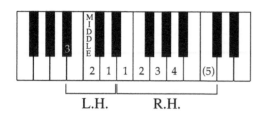

L.H.   R.H.

Words and Music by John Lennon
and Paul McCartney

Sweetly, dreamily

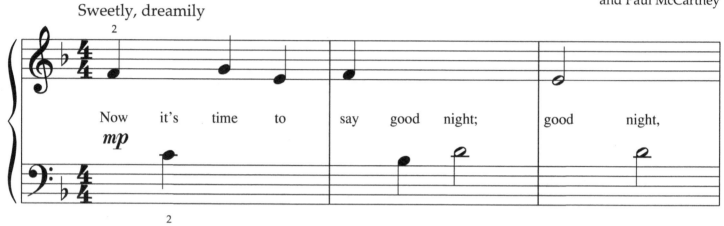

Now it's time to say good night; good night,

sleep tight. Now the sun turns out his light;

Duet Part (Student plays one octave higher than written.)
Sweetly, dreamily

With pedal

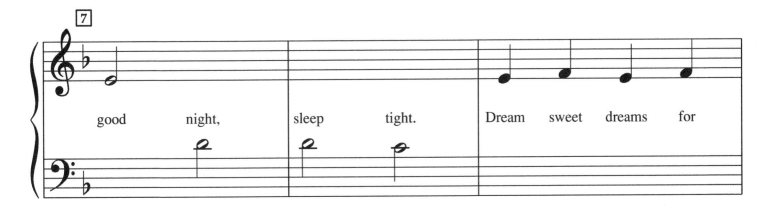

good night, sleep tight. Dream sweet dreams for

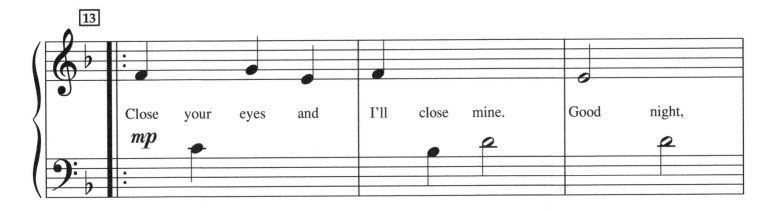

me, dream sweet dreams for you. *p*

Close your eyes and I'll close mine. Good night,

mp

pp *p*

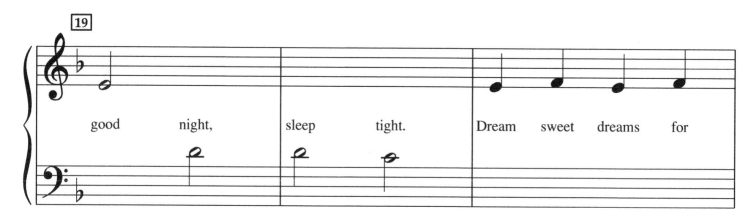

24

Here Comes the Sun

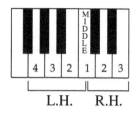

Words and Music by
George Harrison

Brightly

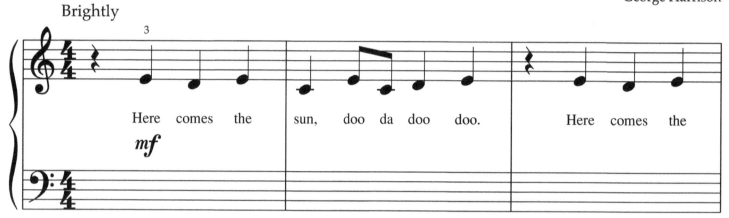

Here comes the sun, doo da doo doo. Here comes the

mf

sun, and I say, "It's all right." ___

Duet Part (Student plays one octave higher than written.)

Brightly

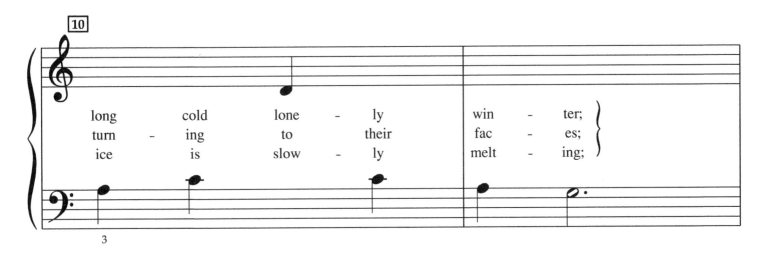

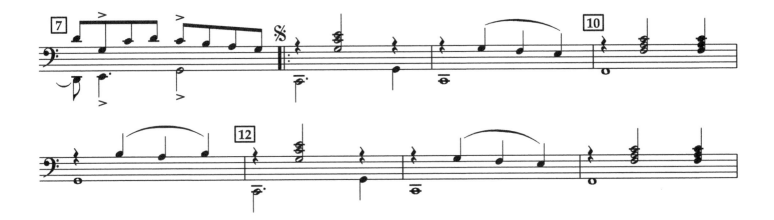

here.

Here comes the sun.

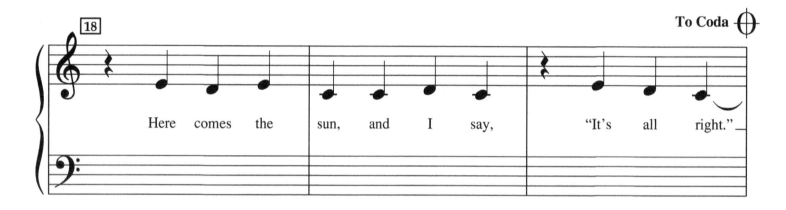

To Coda ⊕

Here comes the sun, and I say, "It's all right."

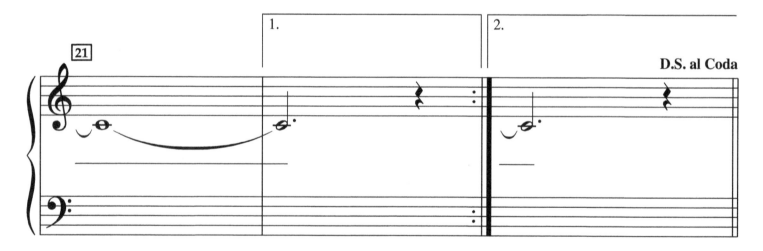

1.

2.

D.S. al Coda

To Coda ⊕

1.

2.

D.S. al Coda

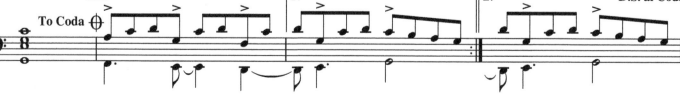

CODA

Here comes the sun,

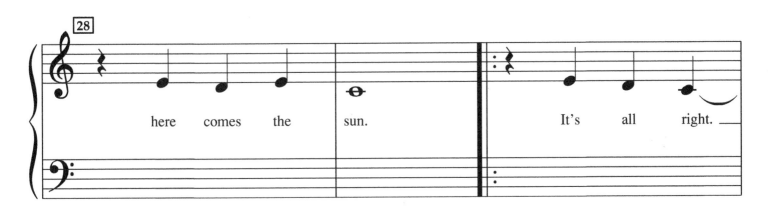

here comes the sun.   It's all right.

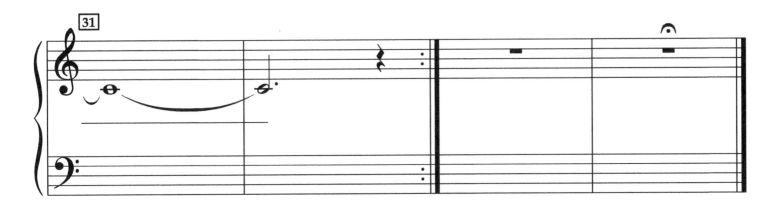

CODA

I Saw Her Standing There

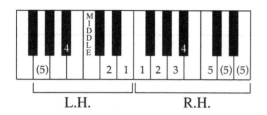

Words and Music by John Lennon
and Paul McCartney

Steady bright Rock beat

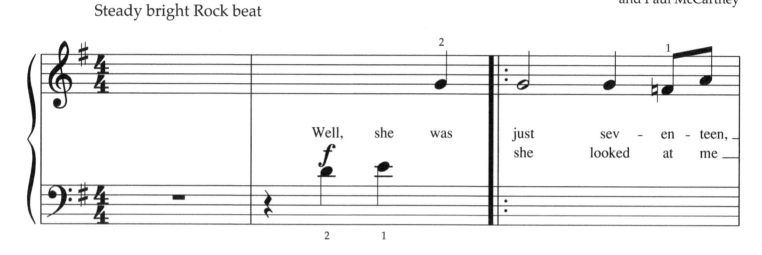

Duet Part (Student plays one octave higher than written.)
Steady bright Rock beat

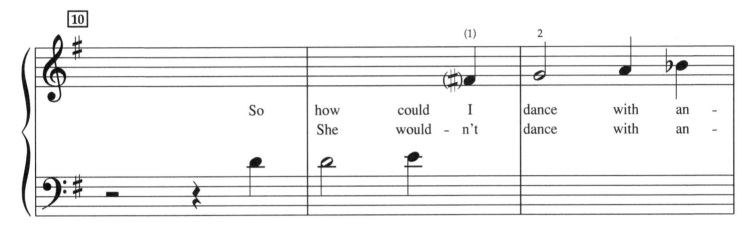

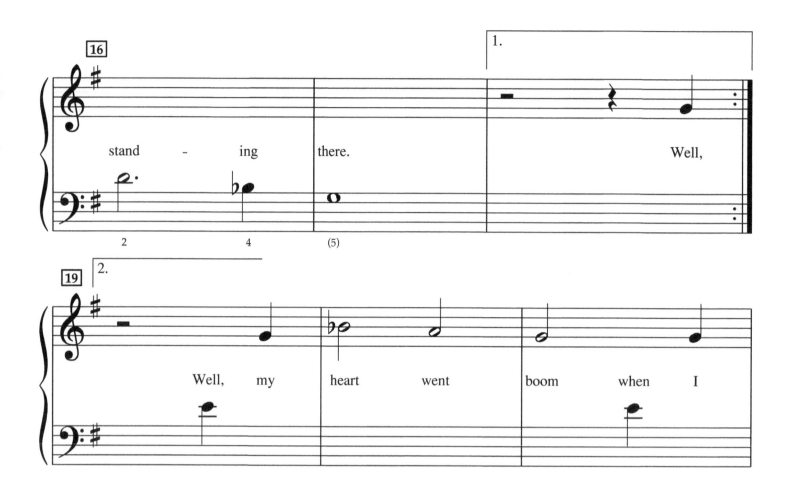

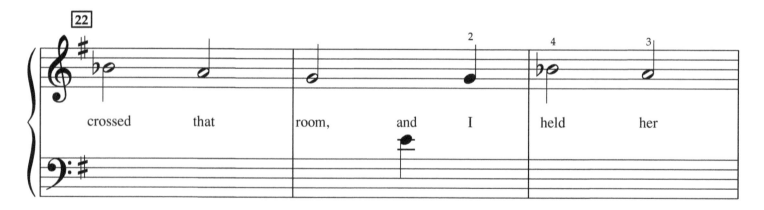

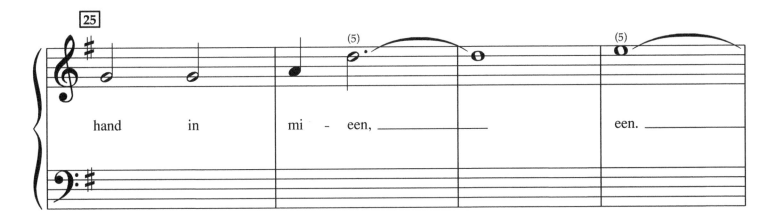

hand   in   mi - een,   een.

         Well,   we   danced   through   the   night   and we

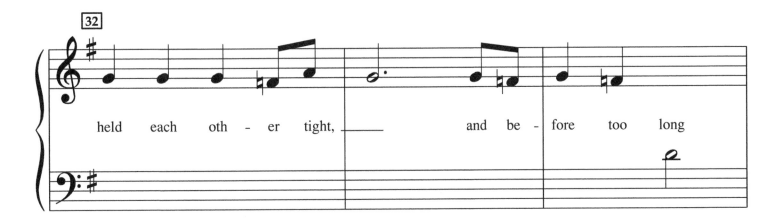

held   each   oth – er   tight,   and be - fore   too   long

I fell in love with her. _____ Now

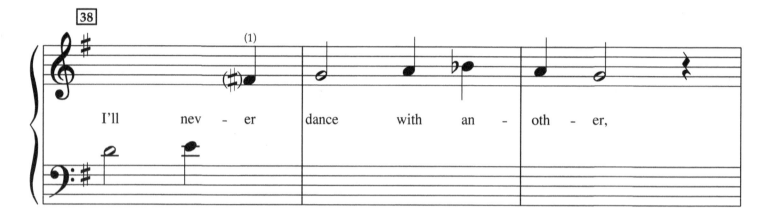

I'll nev - er dance with an - oth - er,

oh, since I saw her stand - ing

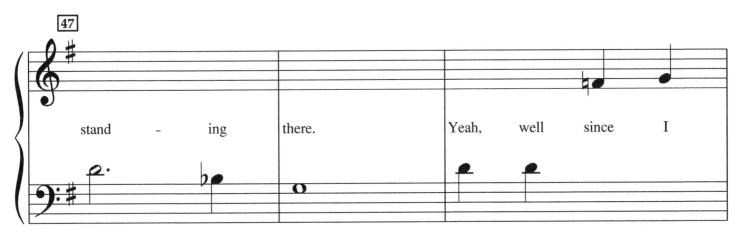

(5)

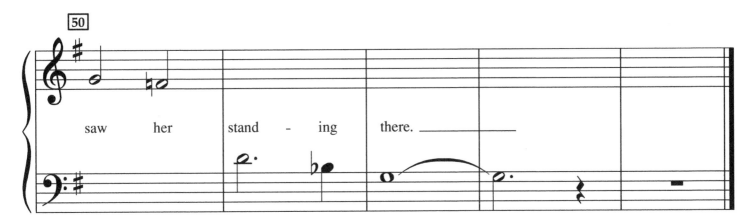

Michelle

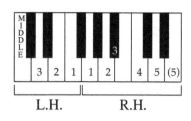

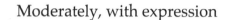

L.H.   R.H.

Words and Music by John Lennon
and Paul McCartney

Moderately, with expression

Mi - chelle,   ma belle,   these are words that

go to - geth - er   well,   my Mi - chelle.

Duet Part (Student plays one octave higher than written.)
Moderately, with expression

With pedal

Mi - chelle, ma belle, sont des mots qui
Mi - chelle, ma belle, sont des mots qui

mp

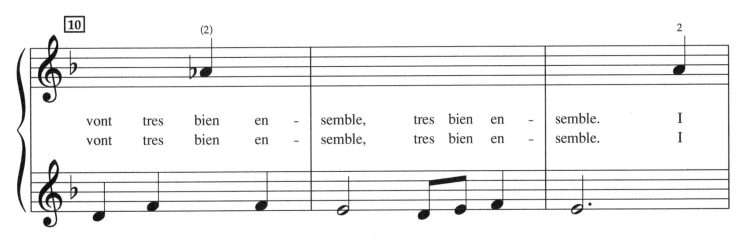

vont tres bien en - semble, tres bien en - semble. I
vont tres bien en - semble, tres bien en - semble. I

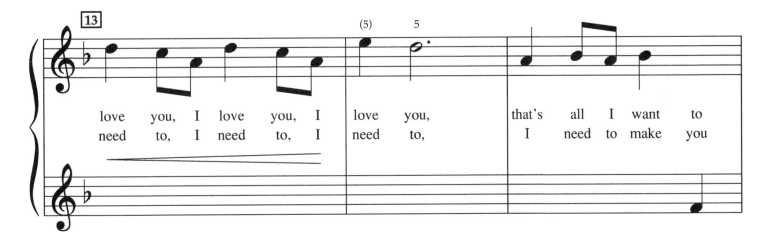

love you, I love you, I love you, that's all I want to
need to, I need to, I need to, I need to make you

say. Un - til I find a way, ___ I will
see. Oh, what you mean to me. ___ Un -

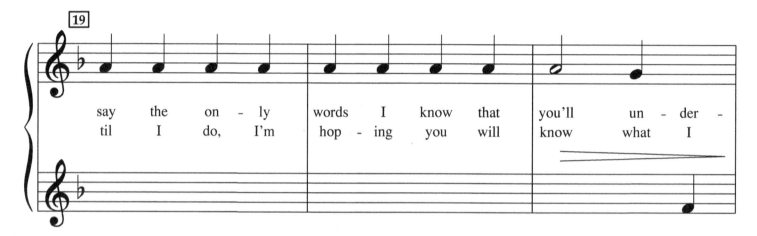

say the on - ly words I know that you'll un - der -
til I do, I'm hop - ing you will know what I

1.

2.

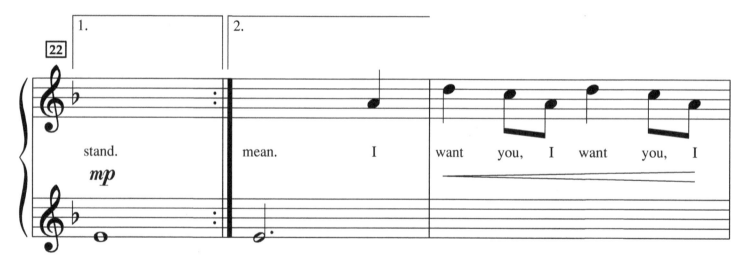

stand.

mean. I want you, I want you, I

mp

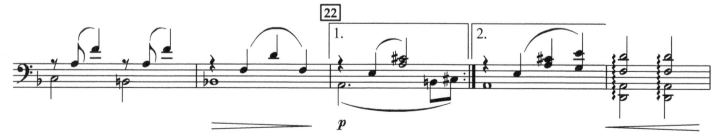

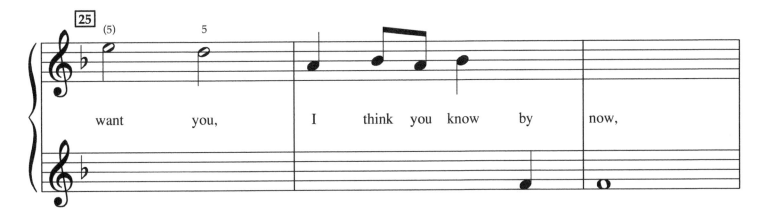

want you, I think you know by now,

I'll get to you some - how. _____ Un - til I do, I'm

tell - ing you, so you'll un - der - stand. Mi - chelle,

ma belle, sont des mots qui vont tres bien en - semble, tres bien en -

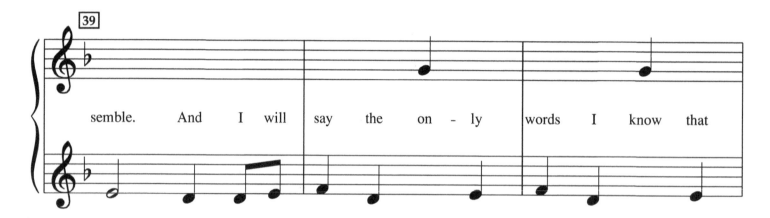

semble. And I will say the on - ly words I know that

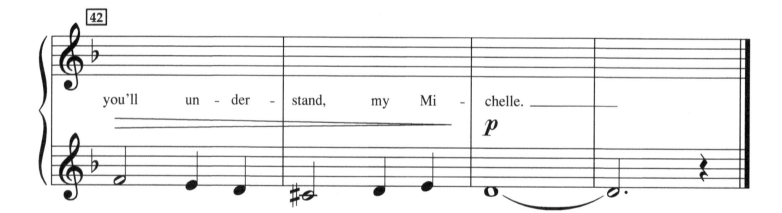

you'll un - der - stand, my Mi - chelle. _____

p

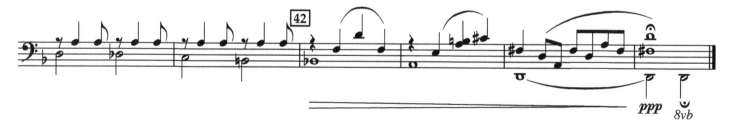

ppp *8vb*